Let's Choose Peace!

By

Lucas Wesley-Buckley

Everyone in the world should choose peace!

Wars should stop.

Everyone could go safely to their home. They could be happy.

Can you be friends with someone whose skin is different than yours?

Yes, of course you can! It doesn't matter what people look like. It only matters how they act.

If someone says you can't be friends with someone different than you, they are a liar. You do not have to listen to them. You can be friends with everyone!

You can play with girls or boys. I like to play and share with all my friends. I have fun with girls and with boys. Some of my friends have dark skin; I love them and share with them too.

If somebody uses a wheelchair, you

can still be friends with them too!

Be nice and friendly to them the

same as other people.

It's OK if people are different from you. If they speak a different language, I still will be friends with them.

We should all choose peace. Even bad people could change by thinking about how to be good. We should help them change and be nice to them.

We should not shoot guns,
or throw things,
or kick people either.

Maybe people can apologize.
They can share and be gentle.

We should help people get a house if they don't have one. We should also give them food and toys and gifts. It is kind to share.

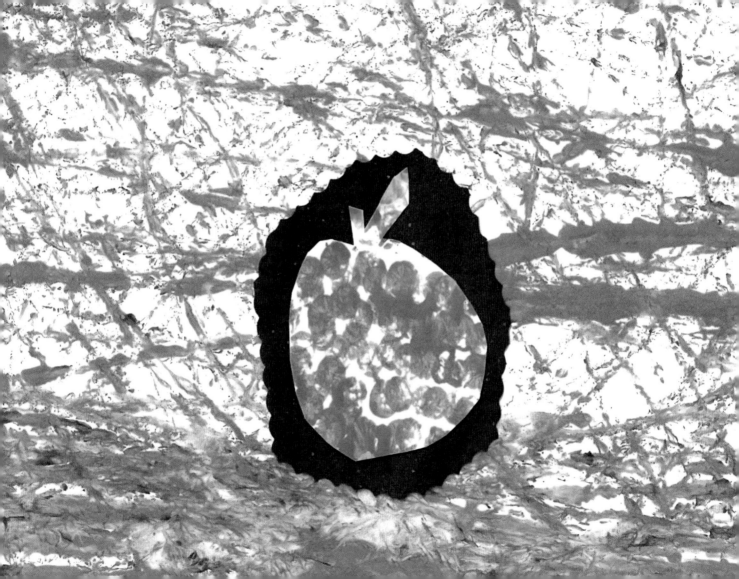

We should also be kind to animals too. Animals don't want you to be rough or mean. We should pet them gently.

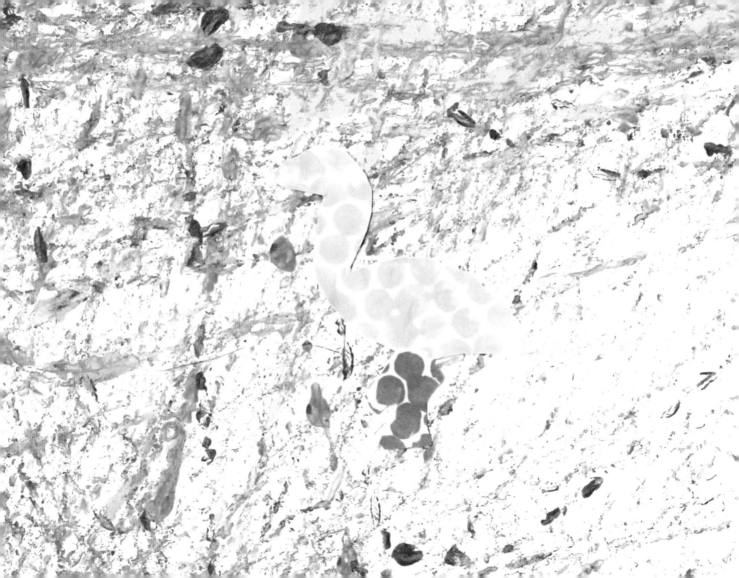

I will never be rough or hit my dog!

She is a nice and calm and gentle dog.

Animals will be happy and safe if we plant more trees.

We shouldn't put garbage in the water. We shouldn't put anything in the water, except ourself when we play on the sand.

We should help all the animals stay healthy that are in the ocean and on land.

I'm excited for everyone to choose peace! We should help people all over the world. Even in Florida and Maine and Montana. Every state and country.

If someone tries to stop us from choosing peace I will shout "Never!"

I will shout it loudly, if my sister is not napping.

They can't make us do bad things. Even if they try to, I will do nothing but good things. We will all choose peace all over the world and spread peace to everyone! Be nice to everyone!

We can start choosing peace right now! Everyone can choose peace. People do not need to wait to start choosing peace. Even if you didn't before, now is a good time to start. Let's all choose peace everyday!

Peace is made of :

Joy

Calm

Forgiveness

Love

Patience

How to spread peace:

Share

Forgive

Help

Learn

About the Author:

Lucas Wesley-Buckley is 3 years old and lives in Naperville, Illinois with his family and many pets. He is an avid reader, a big fan of math, and a wonderful son and brother. Lucas is excited for the day when there is peace on earth and asks for everyone to choose peace each and every day!

Lucas created the art in this book with paint, marbles and bubble wrap.

Made in the USA
Monee, IL
23 February 2022